contents

foreword from Breast Cancer Campaign

Thank you for buying this book – your reward will be many wonderful eating moments. A recipe is a list of ingredients that, when mixed together in a certain way, provides something wonderful to eat. You have done something wonderful as well, before you have even tried out your first recipe, by generating money for the vital work of the Breast Cancer Campaign.

One woman in nine in the United Kingdom will suffer from breast cancer during her lifetime – that's somone's grandmother, mother, daughter, sister or wife. The Breast Cancer Campaign believes that research is the only way forward if we are to prevent 13,100 women dying from breast cancer every year, and spare their families and friends the distress of losing a loved one.

You are helping to do something about that. Our aim is to 'Research the Cure' by funding research which looks at improving diagnosis and treatment of breast cancer, better understanding of how it develops and, ultimately, either curing the disease or preventing it. All the money raised by sales of this book will go towards research into breast cancer.

We are delighted to be working with Billington's on this project. We would like to thank them and wish you many hours of delicious eating.

Pamela Goldberg
Chief Executive, Breast Cancer Campaign

foreword from Billington's

Although unrefined sugars supplied by Billington's appear on the shelves of almost every UK supermarket, we are not, as you may think, a big organisation. Billington's is a relatively small, private, family company run by a closely knit and dedicated team. Like any group of people, however small, there are a number amongst us and around us who have been attacked by cancer in its various guises. At the time of writing two friends at Billington's are fighting cancer.

Last year, spurred into action by witnessing their mother's personal battle with breast cancer, my fellow director Edward Billington, his sister Suzetta, and his brother Richard ran the London Marathon to raise money for Breast Cancer Campaign. Sometime later, we had the pleasure of meeting the dedicated and inspiring team from the charity and were moved to find a way to generate more money for this important cause.

The result is this wonderful book: a collection of outstanding recipes donated by some of the biggest and best names in the world of food. When we had the idea of asking them all to help Billington's produce such a book, I could not have hoped for a more positive and generous response from each and every one of our contributors. This project borrows their talents and creativity and required their support and cooperation. Our sincere thanks go to all of them.

Sue Lawrence has carefully edited this book for us. Sue, your enthusiasm, commitment and personality inspired our whole team. You have been an absolute star. Thank you so much.

I would also like to thank the Marketing department at Billington's and the Richmond Towers team for coordinating the whole project superbly and just about keeping pace with the tireless Sue Lawrence.

Finally, thanks to you for buying this book and in so doing supporting our fundraising efforts. I know you will enjoy it. Happy cooking!!

Ray Merrick
Managing Director, Billington's   July 2001

introduction from Sue Lawrence

Editing this book has been a joy. But more than that, a great privilege.
I'll admit that liaising with so many cooks has not always been easy. But once pinned down and asked to contribute to The Utterly Unrefined Cookbook, Billington's book for Breast Cancer Campaign, the response was an unequivocal 'Yes', because so many of us have seen loved ones suffer from this dreadful disease. I have been humbled by the moving dedications to family and friends that some contributors have written as introductions to their recipes.

Buying this book not only means you have purchased a unique collection of stunning recipes using our favourite unrefined sugars, but you have also contributed towards the fight against breast cancer.

Thank you so much.
Sue Lawrence

golden granulated

why unrefined sugar?

Not all brown sugars are the same. Many are only brown on the outside: underneath they are really white sugar that has been coated to add colour and some flavour.

golden caster

However, natural unrefined sugars are very simply produced with the aim of locking in, rather than refining out, the natural molasses of the sugar cane. It is this difference that gives unrefined sugars their superior flavour and natural colour. There is an unrefined sugar for every application, whether it's for everyday use, or your favourite 'secret' recipe. Some of these sugars are so often just perceived as baking sugars. In fact, they are a treasure trove of flavours that can make a real difference to both sweet and savoury cooking: often in a matter of seconds. Consider too the wider issues. These sugars are minimally processed, thus kinder to the environment. They are also fairly and responsibly traded, GMO-free and suitable for vegan, vegetarian, gluten-free, low-fat and low-salt diets.

As all good cooks know, the best results are produced using only the finest ingredients and when it comes to sugar, that means **unrefined**

everyday sugars

golden granulated
Ideal for everyday use, unrefined Golden Granulated sugar is the **unrefined** alternative to white refined sugar. Perfect for hot drinks, sprinkling on cereals and fresh fruits and wherever you would use white sugar.

demerara

golden caster
Unrefined Golden Caster sugar has a delicate buttery taste and a fine grain. It should be used in place of white refined caster sugar in all cooking and baking applications.

demerara
With its rich aroma, crunchy texture and golden colour, unrefined Demerara sugar is the traditional sweetener for coffee. Perfect also for topping cereals, cookies, biscuits, cakes and crumbles. Delicious too when sprinkled on porridge and grilled grapefruit.

light muscovado

dark muscovado

molasses sugar

golden icing

sugar crystals

speciality sugars

light muscovado
Unrefined Light Muscovado sugar is the ultimate light brown soft sugar, with a warm honey colour and creamy fudge flavour. It has a richness and depth of flavour which is unmatched by refined light soft brown sugar. Perfect for cakes, biscuits, toffee sauce and savoury dishes.

dark muscovado
Unrefined Dark Muscovado sugar is the ultimate dark brown soft sugar. Its rich taste and natural colour adds depth to all cooking and baking. Perfect for fruit and chocolate cakes, it adds extra depth to marinades, savoury sauces and chutneys.

molasses sugar
Unrefined Molasses sugar is packed full of natural cane molasses and has the deepest colour and richest flavour of all sugars. Perfect for Christmas and dark chocolate cakes, mincemeat and pickles. Excellent also for ethnic cookery, marinades and barbecue dishes.

golden icing
With its mellow, rounded flavour and natural honey colour, unrefined Golden Icing is perfect for all icings, butter-cream, dessert pastry, meringues and cake fillings.

sugar crystals for coffee
Unrefined Sugar Crystals dissolve slowly in your favourite coffee, providing a subtle sweetness and flavour. Also great as a topping on cookies, crumbles and ice-cream.

where can I buy unrefined sugar?

Unrefined sugars are available in all major supermarkets, but not only under the Billington's brand. Confused? It's simple. To ensure that you are buying the finest unrefined sugar, check that it says two things on the packet:

- Unrefined
- Produce of Mauritius

Billington's also supplies a range of organic unrefined sugars. Look out for Organic Granulated, Organic Caster and Organic Demerara sugars.

Try them and taste the difference!

starters

venison salad with peanut sauce and vegetable noodles
Annie Bell
serves 4

With every good wish for Breast Cancer Campaign, for this essential work they have undertaken in researching a cure to this terrible illness.

1 cucumber, peeled, quartered lengthways
  and de-seeded
1 kohlrabi or mooli, peeled and quartered
1½ tsp salt

For the peanut sauce:
1 tbsp vegetable oil
2 shallots, peeled and finely chopped
2 garlic cloves, peeled and finely chopped
1 tsp finely chopped fresh root ginger
½ tsp sea salt
125 g/4½ oz smooth peanut butter
⅓ tsp chilli powder
2 tsp unrefined dark muscovado sugar
1 tbsp lime juice

For the dressing:
1 tbsp Thai fish sauce
1 tbsp lime juice
1 tbsp rice or white wine vinegar
1 tbsp vegetable oil
1 level tbsp unrefined golden caster sugar

For the venison and garnish:
450 g/1 lb venison steak or fillet
oil, salt and pepper
1 large red chilli, de-seeded and finely sliced
1 scant tbsp sesame seeds, toasted in a dry
  frying pan

Cut both cucumber and kohlrabi/mooli into thin strips, place in a bowl and toss with the salt. Leave for 30 minutes.

For the sauce, heat the oil and sweat the shallots, garlic and ginger until they begin to colour. Add the salt, 325 ml/11 fl oz of water and the remaining sauce ingredients, except the lime juice, and work into a smooth sauce. Simmer for 10 minutes, stirring frequently, and then add the lime juice. Place in a bowl, cover and cool.

Combine the dressing ingredients in a small bowl and stir well.

Paint the venison with oil and season it. Heat a griddle or iron frying pan and sear the venison for 1–1½ minutes each side. Allow to cool for 10 minutes.

Transfer the salad vegetables to a sieve, rinse under the cold tap and pat dry on kitchen paper. Toss in a bowl with the dressing to coat and then drain off any excess. Cut the meat into 4 cm/1½-inch strips.

To serve, divide the salad among four plates. Arrange the venison in the centre. Spoon over some of the peanut sauce – be generous but you may not need it all. Scatter over the sliced chilli and sesame seeds to serve.

Annie Bell

caramelised salmon and lime salad
Jill Dupleix

serves 4

This is a particularly irresistible combination of rich pink salmon tossed with fresh herbs in a sweetly tangy Thai dressing of chilli, sugar, lime juice and fish sauce.

200 g/7 oz beansprouts
50 g/1¾ oz fresh mint leaves
25 g/1 oz fresh coriander leaves
4 thick salmon fillets, around 175 g/6 oz each
2 tbsp vegetable oil

For the sauce:
1 small red chilli
3 cm/1¼-inch piece of fresh root ginger, peeled
100 g/3½ oz unrefined light muscovado sugar
2 garlic cloves, peeled and squashed flat
1 spring onion, finely chopped
4 tbsp Thai fish sauce
4 tbsp fresh lime juice

To serve:
2 tbsp salted roasted peanuts, crushed
1 lime, quartered

First make the sauce: finely chop the chilli and cut the ginger into matchsticks. Combine the sugar and 125 ml/4 fl oz of water in a saucepan and bring to the boil, stirring until the sugar melts. Allow to bubble away for a couple of minutes, without letting it burn, and and then carefully add the chilli, ginger, garlic and half the spring onion, stirring constantly. Add the fish sauce and lime juice and simmer for another 2 minutes, stirring constantly. Remove from the heat.

Place the beansprouts in a heatproof bowl, pour boiling water on top to cover and then immediately drain. Combine the beansprouts, mint, coriander and remaining spring onion in a big bowl. Cut the salmon to chunky bite-sized pieces about 3 cm/1¾ inches square and toss in the caramel sauce until coated. Drain the salmon and gently reheat the remaining sauce.

Heat a non-stick frying pan, add the oil and heat. Quickly fry the salmon on both sides (it will colour very quickly), keeping the inside pink, and then add it to the beansprouts and herbs. Pour the caramel sauce over the top (you may not need it all), toss well and serve on warm dinner plates. Scatter with crushed peanuts and serve with lime quarters.

© David Loftus

spiced chicken livers on wilted endives
Tamasin Day-Lewis

serves 6

Tamasin was eager to contribute to this book because, in her own words, 'As I write [in 2001], one friend is dying of breast cancer and two are hoping they've beaten it. I ran the London Marathon this year because I believe none of us can afford to ignore this scourge of our time.'

1 heaped tsp cumin seeds
1 scant tsp coriander seeds
½–¾ tsp cayenne
1–1½ tbsp plain flour
450 g/1 lb organic chicken livers, de-veined, left whole, trimmed
4 tbsp good olive oil
1 tsp unrefined molasses sugar
3 heads of endives (labelled chicory in the supermarkets)
a good knob of butter
sea salt and black peppercorns
lemon juice, to serve

Dry-roast the cumin and coriander seeds in a frying pan until they give off an aroma (about 3 minutes). Place in a mortar and crush with some sea salt and peppercorns and then add the cayenne and flour and blend well. Pat the livers dry and dip them on both sides into the spice mixture.

Heat the oil gently in a saucepan with the sugar. Cut off a couple of rings from the base of the endives and strip the leaves off whole. Melt the butter in a frying pan and, when bubbling, add the livers. Meanwhile, throw the endives into the warm oil and stir gently. Season as they wilt.

Turn the chicken livers over after a couple of minutes (they will be oozingly pink through their spicy coats). Remove the endives, squeeze a little lemon juice over them and place a few leaves on each plate. Check the livers are pink in the middle (not raw) and spoon over the endives. Serve at once.

cured salmon
Jean-Christophe Novelli

serves 4

The curing and marinating process here is the same as you would use to make gravlax. For that, roll the marinated salmon in a mixture of chopped dill and crushed peppercorns and then leave to cure in the fridge for 3–4 days before thinly slicing.

1 kg/2 lb 4 oz rock salt
1 tbsp unrefined golden granulated sugar
1 fillet (1.5 kg/3 lb 5 oz) very fresh salmon

For the marinade:
olive oil
1 head of garlic, each clove peeled and
   roughly chopped
a mixture of torn fresh basil leaves, thyme
   sprigs and bay leaves
5 shallots, peeled and sliced

The day before, mix the salt and sugar. Place the fillet on a tray and completely cover with the salt mixture. Cover with clingfilm and leave in the fridge for about 4 hours.

Make the marinade by pouring a little olive oil into a pan and sweat the garlic, herbs and shallots very, very gently until the shallots are just soft but not browned. Then add enough olive oil to cover and heat gently to allow all the flavours to infuse. Cover with clingfilm and leave to cool and then chill until cold.

Rinse the salt off the salmon and pat the fish dry. Put the cured salmon, skin-side up, into the marinade (ensuring it covers the fish) and then leave, covered, in the fridge for at least 24 hours.

Next day, remove the salmon from the marinade and serve the fish thinly sliced, with lemon juice and accompanied by good bread.

spicy tomato and prawn broth
Lesley Waters

serves 4

I love Thai-style food and the sugar and lime juice balance the heat in this spicy prawn broth to make a satisfying supper in a bowl.

juice and grated zest of 1 lime
1 tbsp groundnut oil
200 g/7 oz raw tiger prawns, shelled
1–2 tbsp red Thai curry paste
400 g can of cherry tomatoes in natural juice
1 kaffir lime leaf, roughly crumbled
200 ml/7 fl oz chicken stock
2 tsp unrefined golden caster or golden
  granulated sugar
110 g/4 oz rice noodles
leaves from a bunch of fresh coriander

In a small bowl, mix together half the lime juice and the oil. Add the prawns and set to one side to marinate.

Place a large saucepan over the heat, add the Thai curry paste and fry for 10 seconds. Add the tomatoes, lime leaf, stock, sugar, lime zest and remaining juice. Bring to the boil and simmer for 10–12 minutes.

Cook the noodles as per the instructions on the packet.

Heat a wok or large frying pan and add the prawns. Stir-fry for 1–2 minutes or until the prawns are pink and cooked. Stir in the coriander leaves.

To serve, divide the hot and sour soup between four serving bowls. Pile over the noodles and arrange the prawns on the top. Serve at once.

main courses

pot-roasted brisket with pancetta, garlic and red wine

Brian Glover First published in **BBC Good Food** magazine

serves 6-8

I was very pleased to be asked to contribute a recipe to this collection in aid of Breast Cancer Campaign. My father died of cancer and, more recently, one of my dearest friends, Fran Little, has successfully battled against breast cancer with a courage, honesty and humour that was both humbling and inspiring. Research against all forms of this dreadful disease is one of the most important health issues of our time. I hope that this collection of recipes helps in the battle against cancer and I wish it every possible success.

1.8 kg/4 lb boned and rolled brisket of beef
90 g/3 oz pancetta, chopped
2 garlic cloves, peeled and cut into slivers
½ teaspoon salt
1 tsp chopped fresh thyme plus a few
   whole sprigs
3 tbsp olive oil
400 g/14 oz baby onions or shallots
450 g/1 lb young carrots
2-3 celery sticks, finely chopped
750 ml bottle of fruity red wine
2-3 bay leaves
2 tbsp tomato purée
1 tsp unrefined light muscovado sugar
salt and pepper

Wipe the meat dry and season it. Mix half the pancetta with the garlic, chopped thyme and salt. Make deep incisions in the beef. Push the mixture in with a spoon handle.

Preheat the oven to 180°C/350°F/Gas Mark 4. Heat the oil in a deep flameproof casserole. Brown the beef on all sides and then remove and set aside.

Brown the onions/shallots and remove. Lower the heat. Cook the rest of the pancetta, two carrots, finely chopped and the celery gently for 6 minutes. Return the beef to the pan. Add the wine, whole thyme sprigs, bay leaves, tomato purée and sugar. Season and bring to a simmer. Cover and cook in the oven for 1 hour 50 minutes. Turn the meat once.

Take from the oven. Add the onions and the whole carrots. Cover.

Cook for 50 minutes, until the carrots and meat are tender. Place the vegetables and meat on a dish. Cover. Leave for 10 minutes. Boil the juices to thicken, season, serve with the sliced meat and vegetables.

sticky ribs
Allegra McEvedy

serves 4

I feel really happy about giving one of my scrummiest recipes to this book. My mum had a mastectomy when I was 14 and it was very upsetting all round. She was so brave and such a good cook, and this recipe is for her.

1 head of garlic
750 g/1 lb 10 oz baby back pork ribs

For the glaze:
½ cup of rice wine vinegar
½ cup of cider vinegar
1 tbsp coriander seeds
½ tbsp cloves
5 allspice berries
1 small white onion, peeled and sliced
2 tbsp olive oil
¼ cup of unrefined dark muscovado sugar
½ tbsp unrefined molasses sugar
½ tbsp Worcestershire sauce
1 cup of tomato ketchup
175 ml/6 fl oz dark beer

Preheat the oven to 180°C/350°F/Gas Mark 4. Roast the whole bulb of garlic for about 15 minutes until it is beginning to squidge when pressed. Turn down the oven to 150°C/300°F/Gas Mark 2.

Put the ribs in a deep roasting tin and cover with water. Put on the hob and bring to just below simmering, i.e. steaming. Leave like this for 30 minutes.

Put the vinegars and spices in a pan and reduce to half the previous volume. Sauté the onion in the olive oil until soft. Once the onion is soft, add the remaining glaze ingredients. Bring up to a simmer and then add the spicy vinegar reduction. Carry on reducing to a glaze consistency. Then purée in the blender, with the peeled, roasted cloves of garlic.

Tip most of the water out of the roasting tin but leave about 1 cm/ ½ inch to stop the glaze from catching. Give the ribs a hefty glaze and whack them in the oven. Cook them for about 1–1½ hours, re-glazing them three or four times during this period.

Serve with a home-made slaw.

moroccan-style chicken parcels
Frances Bissell

serves 6

I am delighted and honoured that you have asked me to contribute a recipe to your fund-raising recipe book for Breast Cancer Campaign. This is such an important and worthwhile venture that if I thought it would help you raise more money, I would donate all my recipes.

6 eggs
200 ml/7 fl oz strong chicken stock
700 g/1 lb 9 oz cooked chicken, off the
  bone, chopped
75–100 g/2¾ –3½ oz unrefined golden
  granulated sugar
100 g/3½ oz flaked almonds, fried gently
  in butter
½ tsp ground cinnamon and nutmeg
2 tsp each cardamom, cumin and coriander
  seeds, crushed
18 sheets of filo pastry, about 15 cm/6 inches
  square
100 g/3½ oz butter, melted

Preheat the oven to 180°C/350°F/Gas Mark 4. Beat the eggs with the stock and cook gently in a non-stick frying pan as if you were making scrambled eggs. When the mixture has thickened slightly, remove the pan from the heat and let it cool. Stir in the chicken and add the sugar, almonds and spices.

To make one parcel, stack three filo squares at an angle to each other, brushing each with melted butter. Spoon some filling into the middle and dampen the pastry around the edges. Draw into the centre and pinch tougher to make a bundle. Or, fold the filo into envelope or cigar shapes.

Bake for 20–25 minutes and serve hot, warm or cold, decorated with olives, almonds and mint, if you like.

mushroom and goat's cheese polenta pie
Angela Nilsen

From **BBC Good Food** magazine

serves 6

A robust, luxurious main course dish for vegetarians to enjoy on special occasions such as Sunday lunch or Christmas dinner. Even meat-eaters will love it.

For the polenta:

700 ml/1¼ pints vegetable stock
150 g/5½ oz quick-cook polenta
200 g/7 oz firm goat's cheese, such as
    Capricorn
50 g/1¾ oz freshly grated Parmesan cheese
2 tbsp chopped fresh parsley
salt and pepper

For the filling:

25 g/1 oz butter
3 tbsp olive oil
450 g/1 lb mixed wild and cultivated
    mushrooms
1 large or 2 small red onions, cut into thin
    wedges
1 tsp unrefined light muscovado sugar
1 celery stick, sliced
2 tbsp ruby port
150 ml/5 fl oz vegetable stock
285 g jar of roasted peppers, drained
200 g pack of vacuum-packed, peeled
    chestnuts
1 tbsp wholegrain mustard
1 tbsp fresh thyme leaves
2 tbsp chopped fresh parsley
142 ml carton of double cream
salt and pepper

Bring the stock to the boil and add the polenta in a steady stream, stirring. Reduce the heat and cook for 1 minute, still stirring. Crumble in half the goat's cheese, add half the Parmesan and all the chopped parsley and season with salt and pepper. Transfer to a 20×30 cm/8-×12-inch oiled tin (the polenta should be about 1 cm/½ inch thick). Leave until set.

Preheat the oven to 190°C/375°F/Gas Mark 5. Heat the butter and 2 tbsp of the oil in a heavy-based pan. Add the mushrooms and fry for 4–5 minutes and then remove the mushrooms and set aside. Pour the remaining oil into the pan, add the onions and cook for 15 minutes until golden, adding more oil if necessary. Stir in the sugar and cook for 5 minutes, add the celery and fry for 2–3 minutes.

Return the mushrooms to the pan, pour in the port to deglaze and then add the stock and let it simmer for 1 minute. Add the peppers, chestnuts, mustard, thyme and parsley. Add the cream, and simmer for 2 minutes.

Crumble in the rest of the goat's cheese, season to taste and then spoon the mixture into a 25×15×4 cm/10×6×1½-inch ovenproof dish. Cut the polenta into 16 slices by cutting lengthways in half and then across into eight. Arrange over the filling and sprinkle with the remaining Parmesan. Bake for 30 minutes and then grill for 5–8 minutes, until golden.

arabian style sweet and sour chicken
Jane Suthering

First published in **Tesco Recipe Magazine**

serves 4

The vinegar makes the chicken wonderfully tender – and the sugar adds a sweet balance.

950 g pack of chicken legs
200 ml/7 fl oz red wine vinegar
15 g pack of fresh mint, finely chopped
1 tsp ground cloves
1 tbsp vegetable oil
15 g/½ oz butter
2 large onions, peeled, halved and thinly sliced
50 g/1¾ oz unrefined molasses sugar
284 ml tub of fresh chicken stock
salt and pepper
fresh mint sprigs, to garnish

Wipe the chicken legs and place in a shallow container, with the vinegar, mint and cloves. Cover and marinate for 8–12 hours, turning occasionally, in the fridge. Remove from the fridge 1–2 hours before cooking.

Remove the chicken from the marinade and pat dry. Stir the marinade and reserve 4 tbsp.

Preheat the oven to 190°C/375°F/Gas Mark 5. Heat the oil and butter in a wide, shallow flameproof casserole and brown the chicken legs on both sides. Remove from the pan and cook the onions in the pan until tender and lightly golden. Stir in the sugar until melted. Add the reserved marinade and the stock and return the chicken to the pan. Bring to a simmer and then transfer, uncovered, to the oven. Cook for 45 minutes, until tender.

Remove the chicken from the casserole and keep warm in the hot oven while you boil the stock for about 5 minutes, to reduce to a rich sauce. Season to taste and pour over the chicken. Garnish with mint sprigs. Serve with rice flavoured with pistachio nuts and dried fruits – or bulghar wheat, green beans and a simple green salad.

Country Living/© National Magazine Company

cider-maker's pork and cabbage
Philippa Davenport

serves 6–8

Philippa Davenport

This easy and comforting dish calls for old-fashioned pork; I mean the meat of a traditionally raised and fed pig, such as Tamworth, Gloucester Old Spot or Middle White. Modern breeds of intensively raised pigs tend to be virtually fatless, tasteless and tough, in other words, miserable eating. Partner the pork with plenty of mash. I recommend roast chestnuts and apple sauce too.

lean end belly of traditionally raised pork,
   weighing about 1.5 kg/3 lb 5 oz when
   rind and bones have been removed
1 tsp ground cinnamon
¼ tsp ground cloves
grated nutmeg
freshly ground black pepper

For the cabbage:
1.1 kg/2 lb 7 oz red cabbage
75 g/2¾ oz currants
2 tbsp unrefined light muscovado sugar
½ tsp salt
generous ¼ tsp ground cinnamon
scant ¼ tsp ground cloves
1½ tsp caraway seeds, bruised
2–2½ tbsp cider vinegar
a knob of butter or melted bacon fat, if
   necessary
grated nutmeg
freshly ground black pepper

Lay the joint in a sturdy roasting pan or a large Le Creuset buffet casserole. Add the cinnamon, cloves, plenty of grated nutmeg and black pepper. Rub the spices into the meat with your fingers. Lay the joint, fat-side up, on a rack straddled across the dish. Put into a cold oven, set the oven to 200°C/400°F/Gas Mark 6 and cook for 40 minutes.

Meanwhile, shred the cabbage finely into a large bowl. Add the currants, sugar, ½ tsp salt, cinnamon, cloves, caraway seeds, plenty of pepper and nutmeg. Mix well with your hands. Add the vinegar and mix again.

When the pork has done 40 minutes, remove it. If lots of fat has collected, pour most of it off. Swirl the rest to film the sides as well as the base of the dish. If virtually no fat has been rendered, smear the dish with butter or bacon fat.

Tip the cabbage mixture into the dish and turn to coat it with fat. Lay the pork, fat-side up, directly on top of the vegetables (no rack is needed now). Cover with a well-fitting lid or a double-thick dome of foil. Return the dish to the oven. Reduce the temperature to 150°C/300°F/Gas Mark 2 and cook for 2½ hours. Remove the pork momentarily and stir and turn the cabbage once or twice during this time.

Carve the meat into thin slices for serving. Leftovers can be eaten cold, or diced and buried in cabbage for gentle but thorough reheating.

lemon and garlic chilli prawns with rice
Brian Turner

serves 4

I love the smell and colour of unrefined sugars; they seem to have a character all of their own which adds to the quality of a dish. I am very happy to donate this recipe and wish Breast Cancer Campaign every success for their future work.

100 g/3½ oz butter
1 shallot, peeled and chopped
225 g/8 oz long grain rice
350 g/12 oz raw tiger prawns
2 garlic cloves, peeled and crushed
a bunch of spring onions, finely sliced
15 g/½ oz piece of fresh root ginger, peeled and diced
1 tsp de-seeded, chopped red chilli
juice of ½ lemon
2 tbsp unrefined molasses sugar
6 tbsp white wine vinegar
2 tbsp Thai fish sauce
3 tbsp chopped fresh coriander

Melt 25 g/1 oz of the butter in a pan and sauté the shallots until soft. Add the rice and cook until coated with the butter. Add enough water to cover and bring to the boil. Cover with greased paper and a tight-fitting lid and cook over a low heat for 10 minutes, until the water has evaporated. Drain, leave to cool slightly and stir.

Grease four 100 ml/3½ fl oz moulds with butter and fill with rice, pressing down with the back of a spoon. Keep warm.

Melt 50 g/1¾ oz of the butter in a frying pan, add the prawns, sauté for 1 minute and then remove the prawns and set aside.

Add the garlic, spring onions, ginger and chilli to the pan, with 2 tbsp water and the remaining ingredients except the coriander and cook for about 3 minutes.

Return the prawns to the pan, with the coriander, and cook for 1–2 minutes.

To serve, invert the rice towers on to four plates and arrange the prawns and sauce around.

roast duck with cider, cream and apples
Simon Hopkinson

First published in **The Independent**

serves 2

Serve with a sharp watercress salad and some small roast potatoes.

1 fresh duck, dressed weight about 1.5 kg/
  3 lb 5 oz
2 × 440 ml cans of sweet cider
284 ml carton of whipping cream
25 g/1 oz butter
3 Granny Smith apples, peeled, cored, cut
  into large dice
1 level tbsp unrefined golden caster sugar
a squeeze of lemon juice
a splash of Calvados
salt and pepper

Puncture the skin of the duck, using a thin skewer and then place upon an inverted bowl in the sink. Fully drench in boiling water from the kettle. (Those little holes open up on contact with the boiling water so the subcutaneous layer of fat beneath can flow out as it cooks later.) The bird should then be allowed to dry on a wire rack or hung from a meat hook: overnight gives best results.

Preheat the oven to 230°C/450°F/Gas Mark 8. Rub salt all over the duck skin and sprinkle some inside, with some pepper. Place the duck on a wire rack inside a roasting tin and roast for 20 minutes. Then reduce the heat to 180°C/350°F/Gas Mark 4 for a further 40–50 minutes. As the fat runs into the tin, periodically pour it off into a metal bowl (to use later for roast potatoes). Remove the duck and allow to cool.

Pour the cider into a stainless-steel pan and bring to the boil. Simmer, allowing it to reduce until very dark and syrupy. Pour in the cream and whisk together, bring back to a simmer and cook a little and then set aside.

Melt the butter in a pan, stir in the apples and sprinkle over the sugar and lemon juice. Stew gently, stirring occasionally, until soft. Splash in the Calvados and stir.

Remove each half of the duck from its carcass, place each half duck in a shallow ovenproof dish and pour over the sauce. Cluster the apples as two small piles into any gaps between the duck and the contours of the dish. Return to the top of the oven and reheat for about 20–25 minutes, or until the duck skin is glazed.

pad thai noodles with prawns
Rick Stein

From Rick Stein's **Seafood Odyssey** (published by BBC Worldwide)

serves 2

To make tamarind water, take a piece of tamarind pulp about the size of a tangerine and place it in a bowl with 150 ml/5 fl oz warm water. With your fingers, work the paste into the water until it has broken down and all the seeds have been released. Now strain the slightly syrupy mixture through a fine sieve into a bowl and discard the fibrous material left in the sieve. It is now ready to use.

175 g/6 oz flat rice noodles
50 ml/2 fl oz groundnut oil
2 garlic cloves, peeled and finely chopped
½ tsp dried chilli flakes
10 large raw prawns, shelled
2 eggs, beaten
2–3 tbsp Thai fish sauce
2–3 tbsp tamarind water
1 tbsp unrefined light muscovado sugar
1 tbsp dried shrimps, coarsely chopped
½ tbsp Thai pickled radish (optional)
4 heaped tbsp roasted peanuts, coarsely
  chopped
4 spring onions, cut into 5 cm/2-inch pieces
  and finely shredded lengthways
50 g/1¾ oz fresh beansprouts
2 tbsp roughly chopped fresh coriander

Soak the noodles in cold water for 1 hour and then drain and set to one side.

Heat the oil in a wok over a high heat. Add the garlic, chilli flakes and prawns and stir-fry for 2–3 minutes, until the prawns are cooked. Pour in the beaten eggs and stir-fry for a few seconds, until they just start to look scrambled. Lower the heat, add the noodles, fish sauce, tamarind water and sugar and toss together for a minute or two until the noodles are tender. Add the dried shrimps, pickled radish (if using), half the peanuts, half the spring onions, half the beansprouts and all the coriander and toss for another minute. Serve sprinkled with the rest of the peanuts, spring onions and beansprouts.

hot puddings

© Jo Broughton

rum banana crêpes with warm coconut sauce
Sybil Kapoor

First published in **House & Garden** magazine

serves 4

Bananas, rum and pancakes are three of my favourite foods, especially when cooked together, so they seemed a good choice for such a worthwhile cause.

25 g/1 oz softened butter
6 bananas
2 tbsp lemon juice, plus extra for serving
4 tbsp dark rum
12 sweet pancakes/crêpes
unrefined golden icing sugar
400 ml can of coconut milk
2 tbsp unrefined dark muscovado sugar

Preheat the oven to 180°C/350°F/Gas Mark 4 and liberally butter an ovenproof gratin dish.

Slice the bananas and toss them in the 2 tbsp of lemon juice and 2 tbsp of the rum. Take the first crêpe, place the sliced bananas down the length of its middle, and then roll into a neat sausage. Transfer to the buttered dish and continue with the remaining pancakes. Once all are filled, lightly dust with icing sugar and bake in the oven for 20 minutes.

Meanwhile, put the coconut milk, muscovado sugar and remaining rum into a small saucepan and set over a low heat. Simmer gently, stirring occasionally, until the sugar has dissolved and the sauce has thickened. Add a squeeze of lemon juice and serve piping hot, with the pancakes.

Sybil Kapoor

gratin of exotic fruits
Mary Berry

serves 6

This is a storecupboard fall-back recipe that relies on three cans and a carton. But in season, it is also lovely when made with fresh fruit: I like raspberries, mangoes and pawpaws.

If you do not have time to chill the pudding sufficiently, just push it into the freezer to speed things up; it will only need 30 minutes, and then the sugar can go on and the pudding be grilled.

425 g can of mango slices
420 g can of mandarin slices
425g can of lychees
600 ml/1 pint double cream
110 g/4 oz unrefined light muscovado sugar

You will need a shallow flameproof dish or dishes. Empty the cans of fruit into a colander, drain well and then tip out on to several sheets of kitchen paper to mop up any remaining moisture. Arrange the fruit in the base of the dish or dishes, heaping it in haphazardly.

Lightly whip the cream until floppy and then spread over the fruits to the edge of the dish or dishes. Don't worry if some of the fruit pokes through the cream. Chill for at least 2 hours: the cream must be very cold and firm (or freeze for 30 minutes).

Preheat the grill to maximum.

Spread the sugar evenly over the cream and grill for about 1–2 minutes or until the sugar becomes liquid and darkens. Watch the pudding constantly as it caramelises; the process happens so rapidly it can blacken and burn.

Give the caramel 1–2 minutes to cool and become brittle and then serve.

brigade pudding
Jeremy Lee

serves 6

I like to use Billington's unrefined sugars in these recipes as I find they have more interesting and varied flavours than refined and caramel-coloured sugars.

225 g/8 oz self-raising flour
60 g/2 oz cold butter
90 g/3 oz suet
5 crisp apples, such as Cox's or Egremont Russet
90 g/3 oz unrefined dark muscovado sugar
100 g/3½ oz raisins
100 g/3½ oz sultanas
50 g/1¾ oz ground almonds
30 ml/1 fl oz dark rum
a pinch of ground mace
1 tsp ground ginger
1 tsp ground cinnamon
1 tsp vanilla extract

Sift the flour into a bowl and grate in the butter. Add 60 g/2 oz of the suet and mix with enough water to bring it together. Put in the fridge for half an hour or so while you make the filling.

Peel and core the apples and then cut them into small cubes. Mix together the apples, sugar, remaining suet and all other ingredients and put to one side.

Cut the dough into four discs, making one slightly smaller and another slightly larger than the others. Lightly flour a board and a rolling pin and roll the dough out into discs that will comfortably fit into your chosen pudding bowl (about 1.2-litre/2-pint capacity). Liberally butter the bowl and put a smallish square of greaseproof paper in the base. Lay the smallest pastry disc on top and then spoon on one-third of the apple mixture. Repeat the process with the two equal-sized discs and then put the largest disc on top.

Seal the bowl with greaseproof paper and foil and then place in a pan of simmering water. Cover the pan and steam for 2½–3 hours. Check the water occasionally and top up as required.

sweet bread with maple toffee apples
Henrietta Green

From Henrietta Green's **Farmers' Market Cookbook** (Kyle Cathie)

serves 4

I believe that the great advantage of shopping at farmers' markets is that you can buy in season. So in the summer, this recipe can be done with cherries and raspberries, in autumn with blackberries and apple and in winter with pear and stem ginger.

50 g/1¾ oz unsalted butter

50 g/1¾ oz unrefined light muscovado sugar

4 late-season eating apples, such as Cox's or Tydeman's Late Orange, peeled, cored and cut into wedges

50 g/1¾ oz raisins

2 tbsp maple syrup

25 g/1 oz pecan nuts, chopped

4 large slices of sweet bread (raisin bread or brioche)

Heat a large frying pan and add the butter, sugar and apples. Cook on a medium heat for 8–10 minutes, until the apples begin to soften and turn a golden caramelised colour. Stir in the raisins, maple syrup and pecan nuts and cook for further 2–3 minutes, until the sauce turns dark golden and syrupy.

Meanwhile, toast the bread on both sides. Arrange the bread on a serving plate and spoon on the apples in the syrup. Serve at once.

blueberry, cheese and apple pastries with honey
Alastair Hendy
serves 8

I had two mums. My real one and my best friend's mum. She was there for me through my boarding school years in Sussex while my parents lived abroad. Although she claimed not to be much of a cook, she'd effortlessly throw together great Sunday lunches with all the trimmings without help, a cookbook or fluster. I'm not sure what she'd make of these pastries, apple pie was more her scene. But Pam these are for you – don't laugh. Pam Munks moved on from her home at Finches Gardens on 17 Feb 2001, when breast cancer took her to another world. I miss her.

1 pack of ready-rolled puff pastry
3 Golden Delicious apples
2 tbsp unrefined light muscovado sugar
1 tsp ground allspice
butter
125 g/4½ oz cream cheese
125 g/4½ oz soft, mild goat's cheese
2 tbsp clear honey
175 g/6 oz blueberries

Preheat the oven to 200°C/400°F/Gas Mark 6. Unroll the pastry and cut it in half lengthways. Then cut each length into four small rectangles and lay them all on a greased baking sheet.

Core the apples and cut them in half; then cut each half into fine segments. Lay the apple slices in a bank of overlapping segments across each rectangle of pastry, sprinkle with sugar and allspice and dot with butter. Bake in the oven for 20 minutes or until golden.

Meanwhile, beat the two cheeses together and warm the honey with 1 tsp of water. Once the tarts are cooked, smear each one with a generous swathe of the cheese mixture, top with blueberries and spoon over some liquid honey. Eat warm.

Alastair Hendy

pear and amaretti tart
Peter Gordon

From **The Sugar Club Cookbook** (Hodder & Stoughton)

serves 8

Cancer, in various forms, has paid several visits to my family, but luckily we've been able to send it away again. I hope the following recipe helps to generate much-needed funds for further research and awareness into breast cancer.

This tart is rich and decadent and should be served with lots of lightly whipped cream. It is fine prepared a day ahead.

30 cm/12-inch shortcrust pastry case,
 blind-baked

For the filling:
210 g/7½ oz unsalted butter
90 g/3 oz unrefined golden caster sugar
250 g/9 oz amaretti biscuits, crushed
110 g/4 oz ground almonds
4 medium free-range eggs
finely grated zest of 2 lemons
1 tbsp lemon juice
6 firm, sweet pears

Put the butter, sugar, amaretti and almonds into a food processor and purée to a paste for 45 seconds. Add the eggs, zest and juice and process for another 30 seconds, processing again briefly after scraping down the bowl.

Set the oven to 180°C/350°F/Gas Mark 4. Spread the mix into the base of the pastry case, levelling it out to come halfway up the case. Cut the pears (peeled if you prefer) into quarters and remove the cores and then place them in a circle evenly around the base, pressing them into the mixture.

Cook for 40 minutes in the middle of the oven. If the tart starts to go too brown, cover lightly with a piece of foil. Allow to cool in the tin before removing.

baked walnut tart
Phil Vickery

serves 6

This recipe is one of my personal favourites and I gladly donate it to The Utterly Unrefined Cookbook. Let's hope the proceeds help the many sufferers of this awful disease.

4 tbsp apricot preserve
23 cm/9-inch diameter × 4 cm/1¾-inch deep, blind-baked pastry case

For the filling:
2 eggs, separated
2 tbsp rum
125 g/4½ oz unrefined golden caster sugar
2 pinches of cream of tartar
125 g/4½ oz walnut pieces, roughly chopped
50 g/1¾ oz melted butter

Set the oven to 180°C/350°F/Gas Mark 4. Put the egg yolks, rum and half the sugar in a mixing bowl and whisk well. When the yolks are pale and creamy, whisk the egg whites and cream of tartar (to prevent the whites from splitting), add the remaining sugar and whisk until firm and glossy.

Spoon the conserve into the base of the cooked flan case.

Fold the egg whites, walnuts and melted butter carefully into the whisked egg yolks and then spoon into the case. Bake in the preheated oven until just set – about 30 minutes – remove and cool before cutting. The tart will rise and collapse slightly but this is normal.

Serve with crème fraîche.

fruit crumble
Jamie Oliver

serves 6

This just has to be the quickest dessert to make in the world! Everyone loves it, and you can use whatever fruit is in season. Serve it with custard, cream, ice-cream or mascarpone.

You can replace half the flour with porridge oats or replace some of the flour with chopped or ground nuts. You can even add a teaspoon of ground ginger. Try some orange segments or chopped stem ginger in with rhubarb, or some toasted almonds with peaches or apricots or some sultanas with apple.

I don't add any water to the fruit because it makes its own juice, but you can add a couple of spoonfuls if you like. Also, I never cook the fruit before making the crumble, there's no need.

For the filling:
450 g/1 lb any fruit and berries
2 tablespoons balsamic vinegar
3 heaped teaspoons unrefined golden
  granulated sugar

For the crumble:
225 g/8 oz plain flour
110 g/4 oz butter
100 g/3½ oz unrefined demerara sugar
a pinch of salt

Put the fruit into a bowl with the balsamic vinegar and the sugar, toss and set aside while you make the crumble.

Put the flour, butter, sugar and salt in a food processor and blitz until it resembles fine breadcrumbs (you can also do this in a mixer or by hand: just rub the mixture between your fingers). Don't work the mixture too much as it will turn into pastry.

Put the fruit into a shallow ovenproof serving dish. Sprinkle the crumble mix over the fruit. Give the dish a bit of a shake and bake it in the oven at about 200°C/400°F/Gas Mark 6 for about half an hour, or until the top is evenly golden. If it starts to go too dark round the edge, turn the oven down a little.

pear eau-de-vie
Antony Worrall Thompson

© Antony Worrall Thompson

serves 4–6

Eau-de-vie – the French liqueur whose name means 'water of life' – is quite potent drunk as a digestif. It may not be to your taste taken after dinner, but works very well with this dish. Poire William would also work well.

25 g/1 oz unsalted butter
2 × 275–350 g/9½–12 oz pears, peeled, cored
   and cut into 6 wedges
3 tbsp unrefined light muscovado sugar
a grating of nutmeg
a pinch of ground cinnamon
3 tbsp eau-de-vie or brandy
1 tsp vanilla extract

Melt the butter in a small, heavy, non-stick frying pan over a medium heat. Add the pears, sugar, nutmeg and cinnamon and cook until the pears are just tender, about 5–6 minutes. Pour the eau-de-vie into the corner of the frying pan. Heat briefly, ignite carefully and shake the pan until the flames go out. Stir in the vanilla extract.

Serve with clotted cream or your favourite vanilla ice-cream.

christmas pudding
Lorna Wing

makes a 1.6 kg/3 lb 8 oz pudding

This is really good served with mandarin butter, made by beating unsalted butter and golden caster sugar together, then adding mandarin juice, zest and some orange liqueur. This can be made months in advance once you have 'doctored' it over 2–3 weeks with brandy.

75 g/2¾ oz plain flour
110 g/4 oz vegetarian suet
75 g/2¾ oz dried cranberries
75 g/2¾ oz dried cherries
225 g/8 oz sultanas
225 g/8 oz raisins
50 g/1¾ oz stem ginger, chopped
2 rounded tbsp orange marmalade
150 g/5½ oz unrefined dark muscovado sugar
3 tbsp molasses
175 g/6 oz fresh breadcrumbs
½ level tsp ground nutmeg
½ level tsp ground cinnamon
3 level tsp mixed spice
¾ level tsp baking powder
½ level tsp salt
3 medium eggs
200 ml/7 fl oz ginger wine
4 tbsp brandy, to douse
3 tbsp brandy, to ignite

Put all the ingredients, except for the brandy, in a large mixing bowl and stir thoroughly to combine. Put the mixture into a 1.75-litre/3-pint pudding basin, ensuring that you leave a gap of 2.5 cm/1 inch at the top so the pudding has room to expand as it cooks.

Cut a disc of greaseproof paper to fit the top of the pudding and place directly on the mixture. Cover the top of the basin with a double layer of foil secured with string. Then put the pudding basin in a pan of boiling water which should always come to halfway up the sides of the basin. Steam over a simmering low heat for 4 hours. If at any time the water level looks too low, top it up with boiling water from a kettle.

When the pudding is cooked, remove the basin from the saucepan and allow it to cool. Store in a cool place.

Over the next 2–3 weeks, remove the foil and greaseproof paper at regular intervals and douse the pudding with brandy. Cover with foil again in between additions. At the end of this period store, well wrapped, until Christmas.

To serve, cover with a new double layer of foil and tie with string. Steam for a further 2 hours over a simmering low heat. Unmould on to a serving dish, warm the brandy in a small saucepan, pour over and carefully ignite. Decorate with holly and quickly bring to the table.

cold puddings

coffee muscovado mousse
Prue Leith

serves 4

This recipe is positively ambrosial. It is so rich in all the wrong things – but on the theory that a little of what you fancy does you good, here goes.

3 eggs, separated
90 g/3 oz unrefined dark muscovado sugar
150 ml/5 fl oz double-strength black coffee
250 ml/9 fl oz double cream, half whipped
1 tbsp rum
15 g/½ oz gelatine
instant coffee, to garnish

In a bowl over simmering water, whisk the egg yolks, sugar and coffee until thick and mousse-like (about 15 minutes). Take the bowl off the heat and whisk until tepid.

Put the rum and 2 tbsp water into a small pan and sprinkle on the gelatine. Leave for 10 minutes and then heat gently until liquid and clear. Whisk into the coffee mixture. Stand in icy water to speed cooling and stir gently until beginning to set.

Fold in two-thirds of the cream. Quickly whisk the egg whites until stiff but not dry and fold them in too. Pour into a dish to set. Use the remaining cream for the top. Before serving, dust lightly with instant coffee.

blackberry meringue chill
Mary Cadogan

Serves 10–12

I am delighted to be able to contribute one of my favourite summer recipes, which I hope you will enjoy making and sharing with friends. I particularly like making this luscious dessert after a day's blackberry picking with the kids.

600 ml/1 pint double cream
50 g/1¾ oz unrefined light muscovado sugar
2 level tbsp cocoa powder
4 meringue nests
450 g/1 lb blackberries, plus 225 g/8 oz
   to serve
golden icing sugar, to dust

Whip the cream until it just holds its shape and then stir in the sugar and sift in the cocoa. Break up the meringue nests into small pieces and lightly mash the blackberries with a fork. Stir both lightly into the cream.

Line a 23 cm/9-inch cake tin with clingfilm. Spoon in the dessert mixture, pressing it into the corners, and then gently smooth the top. Cover and freeze until firm, about 4 hours.

An hour before serving, transfer the dessert from the freezer to the fridge. When ready to serve, turn out on to a flat serving plate, dust the top with sifted icing sugar and scatter blackberries over the top. Chill until ready to serve.

© Sasha Gusov

lemon tart
Rowley Leigh

Adapted from **No Place like Home** (Fourth Estate)

serves 6–8

I am afraid a high-sided tart tin, 22 cm/8½ inches wide and 3 cm/1¼ inches high is essential here. It is also absolutely vital the case is leakproof; after that, it is almost a doddle.

2 lemons
4 eggs, plus 1 egg yolk
150 g/5½ oz unrefined golden
    caster sugar
150 ml/5 fl oz double cream

For the pastry:
125 g/4½ oz unsalted butter,
    diced
175 g/6 oz plain flour
50 g/1¾ oz unrefined golden
    caster sugar
a pinch of salt
2 egg yolks
1 egg
1 tbsp milk

For the pastry, put the butter, flour, sugar and salt in a large bowl and rub together with your fingertips. Make a well in the centre, whisk the egg yolks with 2 tbsp cold water and pour them into the well. Very gently blend the mixture together to form a dough. Shape into a slightly flattened ball, wrap in clingfilm and refrigerate for 1 hour.

Butter and flour the inside of your tart tin. Roll out the pastry to at least 30 cm/12 inches diameter and carefully drop the pastry into the ring, making sure it fits right into the corners and hangs over the edge at every point. Do not cut off this overhang. Ensure there are no holes in the pastry, using excess overhang to carry out repairs. Refrigerate the case for 30 minutes.

Preheat the oven to 180°C/350°F/Gas Mark 4. Line the pastry case with greaseproof paper and fill with baking beans. Bake for 20 minutes and then remove the beans and paper and return the case to the oven for 5 minutes to finish cooking. Beat the egg and milk together and brush over the interior of the case the minute it comes out of the oven while it is still very hot.

For the filling, finely grate the lemon zest into a bowl and then squeeze the lemons well to extract all the juice. Strain the juice over the zest. Whisk the eggs and sugar together until the sugar is dissolved and the mixture smooth. Pour in the double cream, mix together well and then stir in the lemon juice and zest.

Lower the oven to 150°C/300°F/Gas Mark 2. Place the pastry case on the middle shelf of the oven, a third of the way out of the oven. Stir the mixture and then carefully pour it into the pastry case. Slide the tart very carefully back into the oven. It will take 1¾ hours to cook. The surface should not colour: if it threatens to do so, cover loosely with foil.

To test, give the tray a gentle nudge: there should be no sign of liquid movement beneath the surface of the tart.

Allow to cool a little before sawing off the pastry overhang with a serrated knife. Transfer to a plate only when completely cold and then refrigerate.

a very chocolatey mousse
Delia Smith

serves 6

This was the chocolate recipe of the 1960's, but it has now, sadly, been eclipsed by other eras and their equally fashionable recipes. So time for a revival, I think, because it's certainly one of the simplest but nicest chocolate desserts of all.

200 g/7 oz dark chocolate (75% cocoa solids),
   broken into pieces
120 ml/4 fl oz warm water
3 large eggs, separated
40 g/1½ oz golden caster sugar

To serve:
a little whipped cream, optional
**You will also need 6 ramekins, each with a
   capacity of 150 ml/5 fl oz or 6 individual
   serving glasses.**

First of all place the broken-up chocolate and warm water in a large heatproof bowl, which should be sitting over a saucepan of barely simmering water, making sure the bowl doesn't touch the water. Then, keeping the heat at its lowest, allow the chocolate to melt slowly – it should take about 6 minutes. Now remove it from the heat and give it a good stir until it's smooth and glossy, then let the chocolate cool for 2–3 minutes before stirring in the egg yolks. Then give it another good mix with a wooden spoon.

Next, in a clean bowl, whisk the egg whites to the soft-peak stage, then whisk in the sugar, about a third at a time, then whisk again until the whites are glossy. Now, using a metal spoon, fold a tablespoon of the egg whites into the chocolate mixture to loosen it, then carefully fold in the rest. You need to have patience here – it needs gentle folding and cutting movements so that you retain all the precious air, which makes the mousse light. Next divide the mousse between the ramekins or glasses and chill for at least 2 hours, covered with clingfilm. I think it's also good to serve the mousse with a blob of softly whipped cream on top.

Note: this recipe contains raw eggs.

coffee, rum and cardamom trifle
Ruth Watson

From **The Really Helpful Cookbook** (Ebury Press)

serves 6

Trifle seems synonymous with summer, but with its spicy, boozy, toasty flavours, this one's as cosy as a teddy bear – and almost as fluffy.

about 6 trifle sponges
8-10 tbsp dark rum
about 300 ml/10 fl oz whipping cream
1 heaped tbsp unrefined golden caster sugar
8-10 cardamom pods
¼ tsp cinnamon powder
a small handful of toasted, flaked almonds

For the custard:
425 ml/15 fl oz full cream milk
150 ml/5 fl oz whipping or double cream
8 large free-range egg yolks
115 g/4 oz unrefined golden caster sugar
1 level tbsp cornflour
1 heaped tbsp quality coffee granules

You will need:
6 × 300-350 ml/10-12 fl oz glass bowls or
    squat tumblers

First make the custard. Heat the milk and cream in a saucepan until just below simmering point. Meanwhile, whiz the egg yolks, sugar and cornflour together in a food processor until the mixture is thick, creamy and paler than when you started. Take the milk off the heat, pour it on to the egg mixture and pulse for just long enough to blend – the custard should not be too aerated and bubbly.

Quickly but thoroughly rinse out the milk pan and pour the custard back in. Return the saucepan to a medium high heat and bring the contents to the boil, whisking almost continuously. Still whisking, reduce the heat and simmer the thickened custard for 1 minute. Tip in the coffee granules and stir for a few seconds until dissolved. Remove the pan from the heat and plunge the base into ice-cold water. Continue whisking for 2-3 minutes until the custard has cooled a little and then leave it to cool completely, stirring occasionally.

Arrange the trifle sponges in the bottom of the glasses, breaking them up to fit (I like a fairly thick layer but it's up to you). Sprinkle the rum evenly over the sponges. Again the quantity is up to you, but the sponges should be fairly damp. Leave to soak for at least 30 minutes.

Whip the cream and sugar into soft peaks. Put the cardamom pods in a mortar and pound them lightly. Remove and discard the husks, and then grind the little seeds into a fine powder. Now gently fold the ground cardamom and cinnamon powder into the whipped cream.

To assemble the trifle, spoon the cold custard over the trifle sponges in a thick layer, and then top with the whipped cream. Finish with a scattering of toasted almonds.

caramel and malteser ice-cream
Amanda Grant

serves 6–8

I am delighted to be supporting such a worthwhile cause that is so dear to my heart, having lost my mother Jenny to cancer not many years ago. Since I discovered Billington's unrefined sugars I use nothing else. Whether I am cooking a creamy ice-cream like this one, squidgy dark brownies or caramelised onions, there is a sugar that suits – adding both flavour and texture to the finished dish.

568 ml carton of double cream
75 g/2¾ oz unrefined golden caster sugar
4 eggs, separated
2 drops vanilla extract
2 × 37 g bags of Maltesers, crushed
2 × 50 g Caramel bars, roughly chopped

Whip the cream until thick, cover and chill. Put the sugar and egg yolks in a bowl and beat together until thick and fluffy. Fold into the cream, with the vanilla extract, and chill again. In a clean bowl, beat the egg whites until thick and fold them into the cream mix.

Pour into a freezer-proof container and freeze for 30 minutes–1 hour, until the ice-cream is just starting to freeze and is slightly thick.

Crumble in the Maltesers and Caramel bars and mix together. Freeze for a further 5 hours.

orange and demerara granita
Henry Harris

serves 8

Using Billington's natural demerara gives the finished granita a richness that I found you can never get with the more commercial brands of sugar. The rum cream adds a necessary touch of decadence.

1 litre/1¾ pints freshly squeezed orange juice, preferably from organic fruit
250 g/9 oz unrefined demerara sugar, plus extra to serve
juice of 1 lemon
400 ml/14 fl oz double cream
a slug of dark rum

Place about 400 ml/14 fl oz of orange juice in a blender with the sugar and lemon juice. Blitz it to dissolve the sugar and then stir in the remaining orange juice. Put this liquid in a shallow plastic container and transfer to the freezer. After 30 minutes, a thin icy crust should have formed on the surface. Break this up with a fork and return the dish to the freezer. Repeat this process every 30 minutes and eventually you will have a tray of light orange ice crystals. Store until required.

Place the cream and rum in a bowl and whisk until lightly whipped.

To serve, take 8 glasses (martini glasses are good) and chill them. Give the granita a final forking over and spoon it into the glasses. Top each with a generous dollop of rum cream. Sprinkle over a hint of demerara for added crunch and serve at once.

thai rice cake
Roz Denny

serves 8–10

Pat (Allman Miller) lit up any social gathering. Stunningly pretty and bubbly, she was a delightful mix of being in control of her life with a touch of enchanting scattiness. She announced a small breast lump as a minor irritation that positive thought would see off. Even her bald head was an occasion for learning about creating elegant African-inspired headwraps. She carried on regardless, planning her future to train to be a Unitarian minister but died 10 days before starting to read for a theology degree. At her funeral I realised that I wasn't the only person who thought of her as No 1 Best Friend. This recipe has nothing to do with her, but is just the sort of pud she would have adored.

200 g/7 oz Thai jasmine rice
1 litre/1¾ pints milk
125 g/4½ oz unrefined golden caster sugar
1 stem of lemon grass
6 cardamom pods
2 bay leaves
300 ml/10 fl oz whipping cream
6 large free-range eggs, separated

For the topping:
500 g carton of full-fat crème fraîche
1 tsp vanilla extract
grated zest of 1 lemon
1–2 tbsp golden caster sugar
berries or sliced kiwi fruit, to decorate

Blanch the rice in boiling water for 2 minutes and then drain. Place in a large non-stick saucepan with the milk, sugar, lemon grass, cardamom pods and bay leaves. Bring to the boil, stirring once or twice and then simmer gently for about 20 minutes until the milk has been absorbed and the rice grains are soft and plump. Stir occasionally during cooking.

Remove the lemon grass, cardamom and bay leaves and allow the mixture to cool. Meanwhile, heat the oven to 170°C/325°F/Gas Mark 3. Grease and line a 25 cm/10-inch cake tin.

When the rice is tepid, beat in the whipping cream and egg yolks. Whisk the egg whites until they form soft peaks and fold into the mixture. Spoon into the tin. Bake for about 50 minutes until risen and golden brown. The top should be very slightly wobbly.

Allow to cool and chill in the tin and then turn out on to a large serving plate. Peel off the lining paper. Whip the crème fraîche until softly stiff and mix in the vanilla, lemon zest and sugar to taste. Spread over the top and sides of the cake, swirling with a palette knife. Decorate with fruit.

butterscotch meringue layers with roasted plums
Katie Stewart First published in **Sainsbury's Magazine**
serves 6

I think that research into breast cancer is really important and so thank you to Billington's for their support.

8 plums
2 tbsp unrefined golden caster sugar
1 cinnamon stick

For the meringue:
4 large egg whites
225 g/8 oz unrefined golden caster sugar
½ tsp white wine vinegar or lemon juice
2 tbsp chopped roasted hazelnuts
284 ml carton of double cream

Preheat the oven to 180°C/350°F/Gas Mark 4. Cut the plums in half and then remove the stones. Arrange the plum halves in a baking dish, cut-side up and in a single layer, sprinkle with the sugar, add the cinnamon stick and 2 tbsp cold water. Place in the preheated oven and bake for 25 minutes or until tender. Leave to cool.

Turn down the oven to 150°C/300°F/Gas Mark 2. Line two baking trays with baking parchment and mark a 20 cm/8-inch circle on each. A smear of oil on the corners of each tray – under the paper – will hold them in place so they don't move when you spoon on the meringue.

In a large bowl, whisk the egg whites to stiff peaks. Add half the golden caster sugar, 1 tbsp at a time, whisking well after each addition. Whisk in the vinegar or lemon juice. Sprinkle in the remaining sugar and fold it in gently using a metal spoon. Divide the mixture between the paper-lined trays, spooning the mixture into the centre of each circle. Use a spoon to push the meringue out to a circle, keeping within your outlines, and then swirl prettily. Sprinkle one layer with chopped roasted hazelnuts.

Place the meringues in the preheated oven for 40–45 minutes until golden and crisp. Switch off the oven but leave the meringues in, until completely cold. Then remove and slide off the baking parchment.

Place the meringue base (the one without the hazelnuts) on a plate. Whisk the cream to soft peaks and spoon all over. Top with plum halves and a little plum juice. Top with the top meringue layer (with the hazelnuts). Chill in the fridge for at least 2 hours before serving.

Katie Stewart

baking

© Gary Moyes

ribbled raspberry and white chocolate muffins
Ainsley Harriott

From Ainsley Hariott's **Gourmet Express** (published by BBC Worldwide)

makes 8

Ainsley likes to serve these with a shot of espresso or a long milky coffee for a luxurious start to the day.

300 g/10½ oz plain flour
2 tsp baking powder
150 g/5½ oz unrefined golden caster sugar
1 egg
1 tsp vanilla extract
225 ml/7½ fl oz milk
50 g/1¾ oz butter, melted
100 g/3½ oz fresh raspberries
75 g/2¾ oz chopped white chocolate

Preheat the oven to 200°C/400°F/Gas Mark 6. Cut some baking parchment or greaseproof paper into eight 15 cm/6-inch circles and push, creasing the paper, into a muffin tin.

Sift the flour and baking powder into a bowl and stir in the sugar. Crack the egg into a separate bowl and whisk in the vanilla, milk and melted butter. Stir the liquid into the dry ingredients with the raspberries and chocolate, taking care not to overmix.

Spoon the mixture into the cases and bake for 30 minutes or until well risen and just firm.

Ainsley Harriott

Good Housekeeping/© National Magazine Company

sticky ginger ring
Felicity Barnum-Bobb

makes 8 slices

A rich, dark and delicious spiced cake crowned with an irresistible golden unrefined icing and slivers of zingy stem ginger.

100 g/3½ oz butter, diced, plus extra to grease
100 g/3½ oz unrefined light muscovado sugar
3 level tbsp black treacle
100 ml/3½ fl oz milk
2 tbsp brandy
1 large egg, beaten
150 g/5½ oz plain flour
2 level tsp ground ginger
2 level tsp ground cinnamon
1 level tsp bicarbonate of soda
75 g/2¾ oz ready-to-eat pitted prunes,
  chopped coarsely
225 g/8 oz unrefined golden icing sugar, sifted
2 pieces of stem ginger, drained from syrup,
  roughly chopped

Preheat the oven to 150°C/300°F/Gas Mark 2. Using your hands, generously grease a 21.5 cm/8½-inch (600 ml/1 pint) round ring mould with butter.

Put the butter, sugar and treacle in a saucepan and heat gently until melted, stirring. Add the milk and brandy and cool and then beat in the egg.

Sift the flour, spices and bicarbonate of soda into a large mixing bowl. Make a well in the centre, pour in the treacle mixture and stir together until all the flour has been combined – it should have a soft dropping consistency. Stir in the prunes.

Pour into the ring mould and bake for 1 hour or until the cake is firm to the touch and a skewer comes out clean. Leave to cool for 10 minutes and then loosen the sides and turn on to a wire rack.

To make the icing, mix the icing sugar with about 2 tbsp hot water to create a coating consistency. Drizzle over the cake and down the sides and then decorate with the stem ginger.

marmalade gingerbread
Carol Wilson

serves 10

Very dark, soft and moist with a distinctive deep, rich flavour, molasses sugar has the most minerals and vitamins of all the unrefined sugars. Using molasses sugar here does away with the need for weighing out messy treacle or syrup. It produces a wonderfully moist, dark gingerbread with a superb flavour.

225 g/8 oz butter
225 g/8 oz unrefined molasses sugar
300 ml/10 fl oz milk
225 g/8 oz marmalade
375 g/13 oz self-raising flour
1 tbsp ground ginger
2 tsp ground cinnamon
1 tsp grated nutmeg
2 tsp bicarbonate of soda
2 eggs, beaten
7 pieces of preserved stem ginger, chopped
110 g/4 oz sultanas or raisins

Preheat the oven to 150°C/300°F/Gas Mark 2. Melt the first four ingredients together in a pan over a low heat and then cool. Mix the dry ingredients in a mixing bowl and make a hollow in the centre. Slowly pour in the melted mixture, stirring all the time, to form a smooth batter. Beat in the eggs and then stir in the ginger and sultanas or raisins. Pour into a greased, lined 23 cm/9-inch square cake tin and bake for 1½–2 hours until well risen and firm in the centre. Cool in the tin.

This tastes even better if kept, well wrapped, in an airtight tin, for two days before eating.

date and walnut cake
Clare Gordon-Smith

© Clare Gordon-Smith

makes a 900 g/2 lb loaf cake

Based on a recipe from my mother who originally got me cooking in the kitchen – I think to keep me busy and out of her way; actually I really liked being creative there. Sadly, she succumbed to breast cancer when I was a teenager but she was always very positive about life and living. I think she would be quite pleased I was still cooking for a living. This was a cake she would make when we went on those idyllic picnics you always remember from your childhood.

125 g/4½ oz unrefined light muscovado sugar
175 g/6 oz butter, softened
2 large eggs
175 g/6 oz self-raising flour
50 g/1¾ oz porridge oats
50 g/1¾ oz chopped walnuts
175 g/6 oz chopped dates
1 level tsp ground mixed spice

Preheat the oven to 180°C/350°F/Gas Mark 4. Grease a 900 g/2 lb loaf tin.

Cream the sugar and butter until soft and creamy and then gradually beat in the eggs until soft and creamy. Then stir in the dry ingredients, with the nuts and dates. Ensure it is well mixed. Spoon into the tin and bake for 1¼–1½ hours, until cooked through.

Clare Gordon-Smith

dense chocolate loaf cake
Nigella Lawson

From **How to be a Domestic Goddess** (Chatto & Windus). Used by permission of the Random House Group Ltd.

makes 8–10 slices

I think this is the essence of all that is desirable in chocolate: its dark intensity isn't toyed with, nor upstaged by any culinary elaboration. This is the plainest of plain loaf cakes – but that doesn't convey the damp, heady aromatic denseness of it. To understand that, you just have to cook it. And as you'll see, that isn't hard at all.

225 g/8 oz soft unsalted butter
375 g/13 oz dark muscovado sugar
2 large eggs, beaten
1 tsp vanilla extract
100 g/3½ oz best dark chocolate, melted
200 g/7 oz plain flour
1 tsp bicarbonate of soda
23 × 13 × 7 cm/9 × 5 × 3 inch loaf tin

Preheat the oven to Gas 5/190°C/375°F, put in a baking sheet in case of sticky drops later. Grease and line the loaf tin. The lining is important as this is a very damp cake: use parchment, Bake-O-Glide or one of those loaf-tin-shaped paper cases.

Cream the butter and sugar, either with a wooden spoon or with an electric hand-held mixer, and then add the eggs and vanilla, beating in well. Next, fold in the melted and now slightly cooled chocolate, taking care to blend well but being careful not to overbeat. You want the ingredients combined: you dont want a light airy mass. And then gently add the flour, to which you've added the bicarb, alternately spoon by spoon, with 250 ml/9 fl oz of boiling water until you have a smooth and fairly liquid batter. Pour into the lined loaf tin and bake for 30 minutes. Turn the oven down to Gas 3/170°C/325°F and continue to cook for another 15 minutes. The cake will still be a bit squidgy inside, so an inserted cake-tester or skewer won't come out completely clean.

Place the loaf tin on a rack and leave to get completely cold before turning it out. (I often leave it for a day or so: like gingerbread, it improves.) Don't worry if it sinks in the middle: indeed it will do so because it's such a dense and damp cake.

dark muscovado brownies
Sue Lawrence

makes 16

Ever since Billington's sent me the recipe for their dark muscovado pecan brownies I have thrown away all other brownie recipes and stuck with this one, which I have altered slightly to suit my fussy no-nut children.

These muscovado ones are miles apart from those dreadful crumbly, cakey so-called brownies we see in this country. They are dark, moist and rich – yet because they are extremely low in flour, they are also very light. And oh so moreish. I tend to bake a batch and have to leave the kitchen as they cool as the temptation is just too great. And then I deliberately cut them squint so I have to 'trim them up' and obviously eat the trimmings. Not a pretty sight.

350 g/12 oz dark chocolate (60–70% cocoa solids)
250 g/9 oz unsalted butter
3 large free-range eggs
250 g/9 oz unrefined dark muscovado sugar
50 g/1¾ oz plain flour
1 tsp baking powder

Melt the chocolate and butter together and then stir and cool slightly.

Whisk the eggs until pale and then beat in the sugar, stirring well until thick and glossy. Gently fold in the melted chocolate mixture and then sieve in the flour and baking powder.

Pour into a buttered 23 cm/9-inch square cake tin and bake at 170°C/325°F/Gas Mark 3 for about 35 minutes: test by inserting a wooden cocktail stick into the middle. There should be a few moist crumbs adhering.

Remove and cool the tin on a wire rack. After at least 30 minutes, cut and remove to a wire rack to finish cooling.

gooseberry sauce cake
Sophie Grigson

serves 8–10

This is based on American apple sauce cakes so, in the autumn try it again, replacing the gooseberries with home-made apple sauce. It also works brilliantly with rhubarb compote or even stewed plums. If you use sweetened stewed fruit, use only 60 g/2 oz of sugar but, if the fruit is unsweetened, increase it to 110 g/4 oz.

285 g/10 oz self-raising flour
1 tsp baking powder
½ tsp salt
60–110 g/2–4 oz unrefined golden caster sugar
110 g/4 oz unrefined demerara sugar, plus extra for sprinkling
110 g/4 oz butter, melted
2 eggs
400 ml/10 fl oz unsweetened stewed gooseberries
1 tsp vanilla extract

Preheat the oven to 180°C/350°F/Gas Mark 4. Line the base of a 23 cm/9-inch cake tin with non-stick baking parchment and butter the sides.

Mix the flour with the baking powder, salt and the two sugars. Make a well in the centre and add the butter, eggs, stewed gooseberries and vanilla extract. Beat the whole lot together well and then pour into the tin. Smooth down lightly and then sprinkle another 1½–2 tbsp demerara sugar evenly over the surface. Bake for about 45 minutes until firm to the touch. Test by piercing the centre with a skewer. If it comes out clean, the cake is done. Let the cake cool for at least 15 minutes in the tin before turning out.

muscovado sugar meringues with lime cream and mangoes

Nick Nairn

Serves 6

When I was wee, meringues were a huge treat and I still insist on serving these up in the restaurant in big paper cases. It reminds me of the time when the thought of a meringue after tea would occupy my thoughts all day.

3 medium egg whites
175 g/6 oz unrefined light muscovado sugar,
   sieved, plus a little extra for sprinkling
3 small ripe firm mangoes
6 fresh sprigs of mint, to decorate

For the lime cream:
300 ml/10 fl oz double cream
finely grated zest of 2 limes
3 tbsp lime juice (about 1½ limes)
1 tbsp unrefined golden caster sugar

Preheat the oven to 110°C/225°F/Gas Mark ¼. Line a large baking sheet with non-stick baking parchment. Whisk the egg whites in a large, very clean bowl until they form stiff peaks. Very gradually whisk in the sugar, a spoonful at a time, making sure that you whisk the mixture well between each addition to ensure that the sugar has dissolved and combined with the egg whites. This is important in order to prevent the meringues from losing all their volume as muscovado sugar is quite moist and heavy. Spoon the mixture into six meringue shapes on the baking sheet and sprinkle the tops with a little more sugar. Bake for at least 4 hours until very dry and hard. Cool and set aside.

To serve, peel the mangoes, slice the flesh away from either side of the thin, flat stone in the centre. Cut each piece lengthways into long, thin slices.

Whip the cream with the lime zest and sugar until it forms soft peaks. Spoon a little of the cream into the centres of six dessert plates. Arrange slices of mango on top like the points of a star and then spoon over the rest of the cream. Place a meringue in the centre of each star and decorate with mint.

light cherry christmas cake
Orlando Murrin

makes a 20 cm/8-inch cake; cuts into 14 slices

I use unrefined sugar for all my baking. I loved golden caster sugar the moment I found it, but golden icing sugar is something else – it smells almost too delicious to bake with! This cake is a family favourite: the recipe was originally American and baked in a loaf tin; everyone likes their own recipe but I don't believe this can be bettered.

250 g/9 oz butter, softened
200 g/7 oz unrefined light muscovado sugar
4 eggs
200 g/7 oz plain flour
300 g/10½ oz currants
85 g/3 oz pecans, chopped
170 g packet of dried berries (cranberries, blueberries, cherries)
200 g/7 oz glacé cherries, quartered
100 g/3½ oz whole mixed citrus peel, chopped
½ tsp freshly grated nutmeg
1½ tsp ground cinnamon
3 tbsp whisky or brandy

To decorate:
3 tbsp apricot jam
8 glacé cherries
unrefined golden caster sugar, for frosting
whole citrus peel, cut into slices
pecans, halved
thin red ribbon

Preheat the oven to 150°C/300°F/Gas Mark 2. Grease and line a deep 20 cm/8-inch cake tin.

Cream the butter with the sugar until soft and then beat in the eggs one at a time. Then fold in the flour. Tip in the currants, nuts, dried berries, glacé cherries, citrus peel, nutmeg and cinnamon. Stir in the whisky or brandy, mix well and spoon into the tin. Flatten the mixture with the back of a spoon before tapping sharply on a worktop to settle the contents. Then make a smooth depression in the centre of the mixture to help it rise evenly. Bake for 1 hour.

Cover loosely with foil and bake for a further hour, until a skewer comes out clean. Leave in the tin for 30 minutes to cool and then turn out with the paper still on. Once cold, remove the paper, re-wrap in clingfilm and keep in an airtight tin.

To finish, dissolve the jam in 2 tbsp water in a small pan. Press the mixture through a sieve and brush the top of the cake generously with the glaze. Roll the glacé cherries in a little caster sugar and arrange, with citrus peel slices and a few pecan halves, on the cake so they stick to the glaze. Glaze the nuts, and then tie the ribbon round the cake.

Orlando Murrin

bits & pieces

© Richard Haughton

organic ginger and seville orange marmalade with whisky
Thane Prince
makes about 2.7 kg/6 lb

■ love making marmalade. I find that being in the kitchen – with the heady smell of citrus and the brilliant colour – is the perfect antidote to the January cold.

1.25 kg/2 lb 12 oz Seville oranges,
  preferably organic
110 g/4 oz fresh root ginger, preferably
  organic, peeled
1.6 kg/3 lb 8 oz organic unrefined
  caster sugar
1 jar of preserved ginger in syrup
125 ml/4 fl oz whisky

Put the oranges and ginger in a heavy pan with 2.25 litres/4 pints of water and cook until the fruit is soft. Remove both from the pan. Measure and make up the liquid to 1.7 litres/3 pints. Add the sugar.

Cut the orange peel into thin strips. Tie the pith and pips in muslin. Finely shred the boiled ginger. Add all these to the pan along with the strips of peel. Boil for 10 minutes and then add the ginger syrup and finely sliced preserved ginger. Cook until a set is achieved and then stir in the whisky and pot in the usual manner.

sweet chilli jam
Fran Warde

makes 2 small jars

This is not a jam to spread on your toast at breakfast. I call it Asian ketchup, as in that far-flung place huge bottles are served with all savoury meals. Take this warning from me, it is addictive.

Serve it with spring rolls, Thai crab cakes, all griddled or barbecued meats and fish, or use it to accompany cold meats or add a spoonful at the end of cooking to stir-fries. Tempted? Then get cooking; it is easy.

125 g/4½ oz fresh red chillies
1 onion, peeled
5 cm/2-inch piece of fresh root ginger
3 garlic cloves, peeled
125 ml/4 fl oz white vinegar
500 g/1 lb 2 oz unrefined golden caster sugar

Roughly chop all the vegetables, using a small blender and then chop to a fine mince.

Place the vegetables, vinegar, 100 ml/3½ fl oz of water and the sugar in a pan and bring to the boil. Simmer slowly for 15 minutes, stirring frequently. Remove from the heat and allow to cool. The mixture will be thick, sticky and jammy.

Larger quantities can be made and stored in the fridge, but return to room temperature before serving.

© Sam Bailey

fragrant stock syrups
Gordon Ramsay

makes 700 ml/1¼ pints

I have many basic sauces, confits and syrups at the ready in all my kitchens. Stock syrup is one of them and because it is high in sugar it keeps a good time in the fridge. It is amazing how versatile a syrup can be and makes such a difference to even the simplest fruit salad. And, instead of sprinkling fruit with sugar that doesn't dissolve evenly, it is better to dress it lightly in a syrup. This is a basic heavy syrup recipe followed by a list of flavour variations which ring the changes. For a lighter syrup, halve the sugar to water.

500 g/1 lb 2 oz unrefined golden
   granulated sugar
500 ml/18 fl oz water
1 unwaxed lemon

Slowly heat the sugar and water in a large saucepan, stirring once or twice. Whilst this is happening, take three thin strips of peel from the lemon (with a swivel vegetable peeler) and add to the pan. When all the sugar has dissolved and the liquid is clear, raise the heat slowly and boil for 5 minutes; then remove and cool. Pour into a clean bottle or jar and store in the fridge. Remove the lemon zest, otherwise it will stain the syrup light yellow.

Flavour Variations

Warm and spicy: add 2 cinnamon sticks, 2 star anise, 4 whole cloves, 4 cardamoms and a vanilla pod to the pan as it boils. Cool and store with the spices for a full flavour or remove after cooling for a lighter hint.

Lemon grass: slit 3 stems of fresh lemon grass and add to the syrup. Use lime peel strips instead of lemon or add about 4 Thai kaffir lime leaves.

Thyme and rosemary: add 2 generous sprigs of thyme and rosemary to the boiling syrup.

Hibiscus and basil: use either 1 tsp dried hibiscus flowers (from health food shops) or 2 rosehip and hibiscus teabags plus 2 good sprigs of fresh basil.

Malibu: simply add 2 tbsp Malibu liqueur to every 150 ml/5 fl oz syrup. Or use rum, brandy, kirsch or any flavoured eau-de-vie.

a soft, fudgy royal icing
Nigel Slater

makes enough to cover a 23 cm/9-inch cake

The colour of warm fudge, unrefined golden icing sugar has a slightly buttery, toffee flavour, rather than the monotone sugar-hit of the white stuff. Despite the fact it has a pleasing flavour and a healthy glow, it might take a while to find approval with the whiter-than-white brigade. You can almost hear the net curtains twitching.

2 large egg whites
500 g/1 lb 2 oz unrefined golden icing sugar
juice of 1 large lemon

Put the egg whites in a large bowl and beat them loosely with a fork. They will break up and start to froth a little. Now beat half the sifted icing sugar and all of the lemon juice into the egg whites with a wooden spoon. You will need to beat for about 10 minutes until it is completely smooth. Stir in the remaining sugar until you have a thick paste. It should be quite hard going to stir towards the end. Cover with a clean, wet tea towel until needed.

blackcurrant jelly
Paul Heathcote

makes up to 100 small pieces

Every ingredient is important. The finest products make the finest food and that is why I use Billington's unrefined sugar in all my restaurants.

1 kg/2 lb 4 oz blackcurrants, liquidised and passed through a fine sieve to remove skin and seeds
800 g/1 lb 12 oz organic unrefined caster sugar
65 g/2½ oz pectin

Mix the blackcurrants and 700 g/1 lb 9 oz sugar together and boil to 50°C. Mix the pectin and the remaining sugar and add to the blackcurrant syrup. Cook to 106°C/223°F. Pour on to large non-stick baking trays, allow to cool, cut into squares and store in organic sugar.

Paul Heathcote

raspberry jam
Marguerite Patten OBE

From **The Basic Basics: Jams, Preserves and Chutneys** (Grub Street)

Twice my family have experienced the frightening news that people dear to us have breast cancer. Happily, after surgical treatment, all was well. I congratulate the Billington Food Group on making an important contribution to research into breast cancer with money raised from the sale of this book.

Raspberries are rubus species within the rose group and I think they have one of the most delicate flavours of all fruits. Raspberry jam has always been a great favourite of mine. Raspberries contain an average amount of pectin and the jam sets without problems.

450 g/1 lb raspberries
450 g/1 lb unrefined golden
   granulated sugar

Put the fruit into a preserving pan and mash with a wooden spoon. Heat gently to boiling point. Add the sugar and stir over a low heat until this has dissolved. Then allow the jam to boil rapidly until setting point is reached. Spoon into hot jars and seal down.

There is one problem with raspberry jam and that is the pips, so make:

Seedless Raspberry Jam
Simmer the fruit and then rub through a non-metal sieve. Measure the pulp and allow 450g/1 lb unrefined golden granulated sugar to each 600 ml/1 pint of purée. Heat the purée to boiling point, add the sugar then continue as above.

Uncooked Raspberry Jam
This is only possible if the fruit is very fresh and perfectly ripe.
Use 450 g/1 lb unrefined golden granulated sugar to 450 g/1 lb raspberries.
Put the sugar into an ovenproof dish and place in the oven, set to the lowest heat, for 15 minutes or until it is just warm. Put the raspberries into a bowl, add the sugar and mash together until the sugar has melted. Spoon into hot jars and seal down. This jam should be kept in the refrigerator.
The jam can be frozen, in which case allow about 2.5 cm/1 inch of space at the top of the jars for expansion during freezing.

rum butter with orange zest
Josceline Dimbleby

serves 10

It was my grandmother who instilled in me a lifelong passion for the matchless taste of unrefined brown sugar, which she used to buy from the first Health Food shop in London in the 1950s. She used it in her rice puddings and her brandy butter at Christmas and I adored both.

In this lovely version of rum butter, the luscious flavours of raw sugar and orange rind enhance both the Christmas pudding or mince pies and, at other times of the year, any hot fruit pie, crumble or tart. My mother, who suffered and recovered from breast cancer, loved my recipe and I am delighted that it should be included in this very special book.

225 g/8 oz unsalted butter
150–175 g/5½–6 oz unrefined light
**   muscovado sugar**
finely grated zest of 1 orange
4–5 tbsp dark rum

Cream the butter with an electric whisk until soft. Thoroughly whisk in the sugar and then the orange zest. Then whisk in the rum, a little at a time. If you use a food processor, simply whizz the first three ingredients together until smooth and then add the rum gradually.

Keep in the fridge but take out and bring to room temperature well before you start the meal. Serve with Christmas pudding or mince pies.

index

The utterly unrefined cookbook

edited by Sue Lawrence

SIMON & SCHUSTER

A VIACOM COMPANY

First published in Great Britain by Simon & Schuster UK Ltd, 2002
A Viacom Company

ISBN 0 743 22110 9

3 5 7 9 10 8 6 4

Simon & Schuster UK Ltd
Africa House
64-78 Kingsway
London WC2B 6AH

Design: Trevor Newman
Photographs: Joff Lee
Home economist: Sue Ashworth
Stylist: Clare Hunt
Typeset by Stylize Digital Artwork
Printed and bound in China